D1716029

INTEGRATING BEGINNING MATH & LITERATURE

by Carol A. Rommel

Incentive Publications, Inc.
Nashville, TN

Cover and illustrations by Dianna Richey
Edited by Sherri Y. Lewis

ISBN 0-86530-215-4

TABLE OF CONTENTS

PREFACE

The National Association for the Education of Young Children in its guidelines for developmentally appropriate curriculum called for:

1. an integrated curriculum approach
2. an interactive process involving children in active exploration and interaction with adults, children, and materials
3. learning activities and materials that are concrete, real, and relevant
4. a variety of activities and materials with increasing complexity

In accordance with these guidelines, this curriculum project consists of 31 units integrating children's literature with mathematics. The math activities are concrete and interactive and can be made appropriately more complex as the children's needs grow. Most importantly they are real and relevant with the potential for jointly inspiring primary children with the desire to read and to apply math to solve problems. Finally, each unit includes key language concepts to be developed during the activities.

Language is an integral part of mathematics concept development and is best emphasized by correct, consistent usage within conversations between fellow students and teachers. For this reason the majority of activities in each unit are intended to be used in small group situations allowing maximum conversation by all participants. The activities follow the whole group reading of the literature and initial discussion of the language concepts by teacher and students.

Note: Language concepts are divided into three categories.

1. exposure concepts
2. mastery concepts
3. review concepts

TEACHING AIDS

"Work mats" or "work boards" are easily made by drawing simple outline pictures on file folders or oaktag. Use a copying machine to minimize your work! You may ask the children to color the pictures. The children will then use the mats or boards as supports for their manipulatives as they work. To make the "apple boards" for the *Johnny Appleseed* unit, p. 11, draw simple outlines of two trees on each board. A "How Much Money" board (*Our Garage Sale*, p. 26) should be decorated with an outline of a money bag. To make Curious George mats (*Curious George*, p. 41), draw a simple picture of Curious George on each mat. For "smile boards" (*Little Rabbit's Loose Tooth*, p. 49), draw a curved line (smile) on the manila folder or piece of oaktag for each child. Draw an outline of a cake to make a birthday cake mat (*A Birthday For Frances*, p. 55), and an outline of a leaf to make a leaf mat (*The Grouchy Ladybug*, p. 65). "Wonderland work sheets" (*Alice's Adventures in Wonderland*, p. 71) are file folders or pieces of oaktag on which you have drawn items from Wonderland such as the Mad Hatter's Teapot, the White Rabbit's Gloves and the Mad Hatter's Hat. The Yangtze River work mat (Activity 2, *The Story of Ping*, p. 73) is made by drawing two wavy lines across the mat.

Activity 2 for *The Biggest Nose*, p. 15, requires "Measuring our animals" charts. Make each chart by dividing an 8½" x 11" sheet of paper into two columns. Write PART OF ANIMAL at top of left column and MEASUREMENT at top of right column (use copy machine to save time if making many charts). Write the name of each animal at the top of a chart.

To make the gameboard for Activity 2 for *The Sandman*, page 30, write numbers from 1 to 20 on twenty index cards (make numbers large). Tape cards together in numerical order and place flat on table or floor. Then make instruction cards, again using index cards. Each instruction card should read "Go up (number)" or "Go down (number)." The game begins when up to 5 children place their counters on Number 10 on the gameboard. Children draw cards and follow the instructions by reading the directions aloud and moving the counters up/down the specified number of spaces. The game continues until one child successfully "climbs back up the mountain with his/her sheep" (moves his/her counter to Number 20 on the gameboard).

JOHNNY APPLESEED

by Steven Kellog

PREREQUISITES

Children should be able to count by rote to 20, recognize basic colors, and have some idea of "more or less."

LANGUAGE CONCEPTS

Exposure – second, decade, hundreds of miles, a few years

Mastery – ordinal numbers (1-10), more or less, same and equal

1 ACTIVITY
Calendar Concepts

MATERIALS

- 1 inch graph paper or calendar outline
- crayons or markers

This book is a good overall introduction to the concepts of time – calendar, days, weeks, months, seasons, and a year. Have the children make a September calendar. Teach a days of the week song and sing it repeatedly during the month. Discuss how each month starts differently each year, and record each day in September as it passes, drawing an apple in the appropriate space. Have the children tape their calendar to their desk or have it readily available. The calendar may be used on a daily basis to practice:

1. counting by rote to 30 (Teach pattern beyond 20 for those who need it.)

2. ordinal numbers 1-10 (Have children practice putting apples on the first day of September, the eighth, etc.)

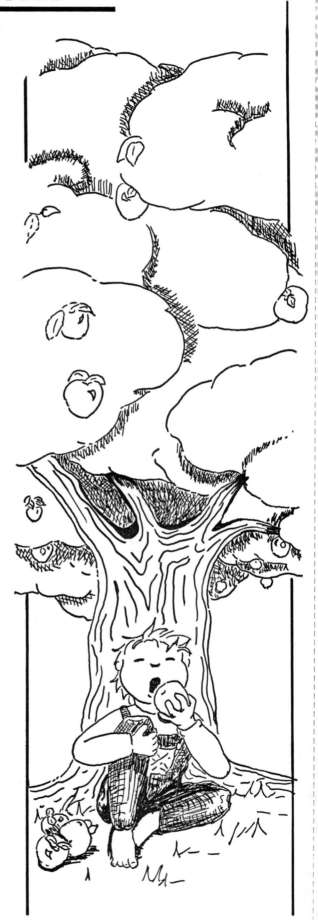

2 ACTIVITY
Comparing Apples

MATERIALS
- flannel board
- flannel pieces for apple trees, Johnny, and his basket

Tell a short story about Johnny picking some apples and leaving some on the tree. Have the students work in pairs. One pair receives items picked. The other pair receives the apples left on the tree. Students lay out the apples in front of them. "Who has the most?" "Who has the least?" "Did Johnny pick more apples or did he leave more on the tree?" The game continues so each child has a turn to leave some apples on the tree and Johnny picks some for his basket. Have the student pairs place their apples in lines next to each other to compare them. Note whether the children:
- use one-to-one correspondence in arranging the rows of apples
- tell how many more one group has than the other

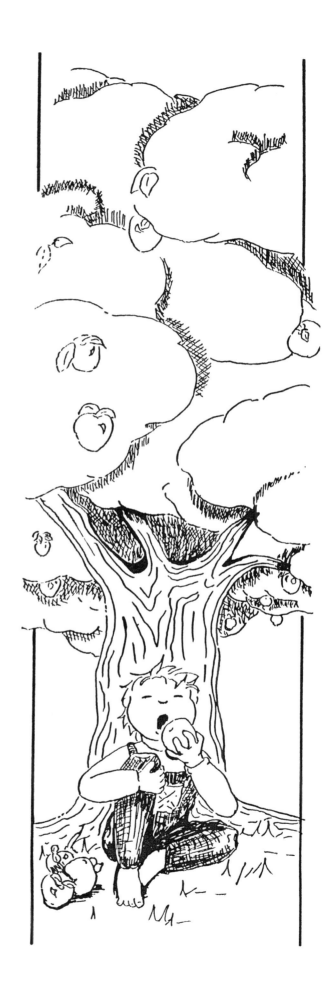

3 ACTIVITY
Interpreting Apple Graphs

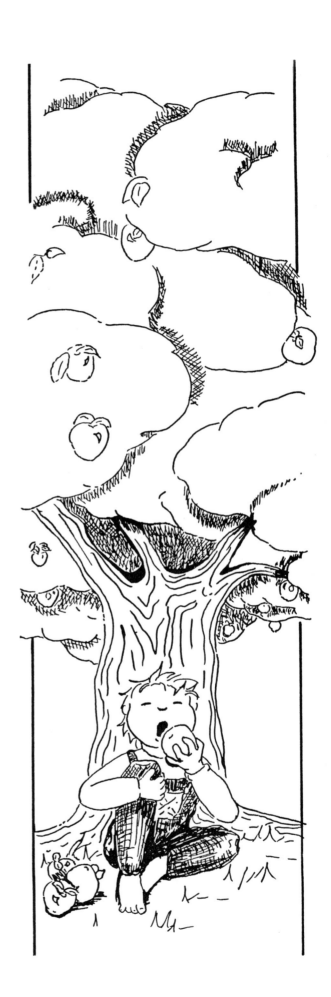

MATERIALS
- manipulative cubes or other concrete objects to use as apples
- minigraphs
- paper cups

Provide each student with a minigraph and two cups of apples (red and yellow). Each child empties his/her apples and arranges them on his/her graph. Following the teacher's modeling, each child discusses his/her graph indicating which group has more or less, how many more one group has, how many less the other group has, how many apples are shown on the graph altogether, etc.

Extension
At another time, students might work in pairs joining two graphs together and using two other kinds of fruit to be sure they can interpret real graphs with four groups.

MATERIALS (Used for activities 4-8)
- apple boards
- real apples, real lima beans, unifix cubes, or any other concrete apple objects
- numeral cards 0-10 (also plus and minus)
- cups or baskets depending on apple objects

4 ACTIVITY
Counting Apples

Give each child a basket or cup of apples. Children sit in a circle and sing a short apple song or other appropriate song. One child skips around the circle and stops at the end of the song. The child whom he/she stops behind empties his/her basket of apples out for him/her to count. He/she then counts his/her apples and states, "I have _____ apples." If he/she has counted correctly, then the basket of apples becomes his/hers and the child whom he/she stopped behind becomes "It." If he/she counts incorrectly, then he/she takes another turn until he/she is successful.

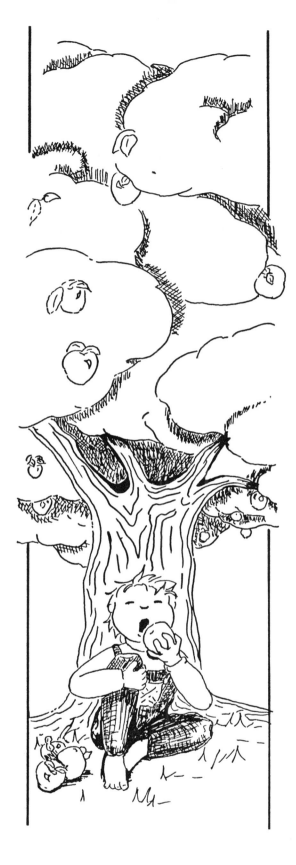

5 ACTIVITY
Matching Numerals To Sets

This activity is played the same as activity 4, only this time the child selects a numeral card to depict how many apples he/she has taken. He/she then states, "I have ___ apples," (and he/she shows the correct numeral beside his/her apples).

6 ACTIVITY
Making Sets With Objects

All numeral cards are spread out on the table. The children work as a group matching the correct number of apples with each numeral. They check each other's work.

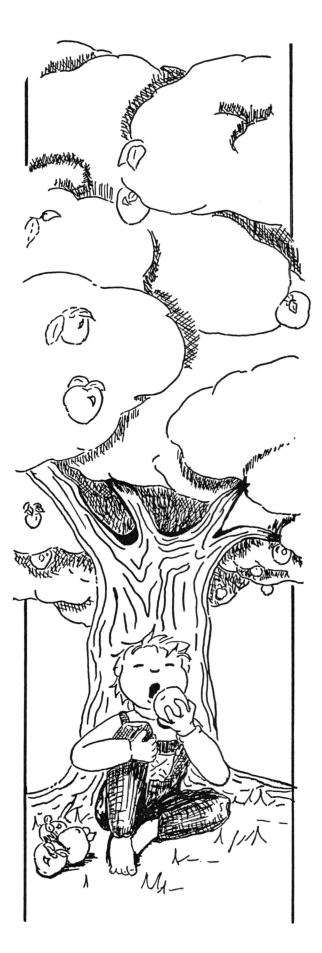

7 ACTIVITY
Counting Apples

Direct the children to put apples on the left tree and apples on the right tree. (Some instruction of the concepts "left" and "right" may be needed, or if the teacher prefers, he/she may call them the "first" and "second" tree instead.) Ask the question, "How many apples are there in all?" Observe to see whether children:

- count all
- count on from first number
- give the total without counting

8 ACTIVITY
Counting Apples/Recording Results

Each child has his/her own apple board, a cup with a specific number of apples in it, numeral cards 0-10, a "plus," and an "equals" sign. The teacher models and instructs the meaning of "plus" and "equals." Each child shakes his/her cup, puts some apples on the left tree, puts some apples on the right tree, and records a number sentence. Continue with all possible sentences for each number practiced. *Example: Number 5 – 1+4, 4+1, 2+3, 3+2, 0+5, 5+0.*

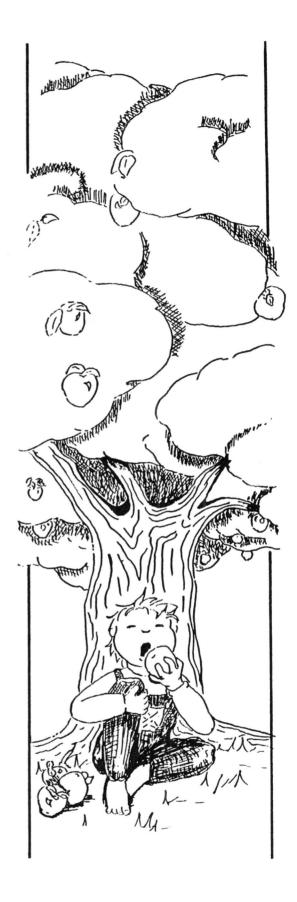

GOING TO THE DOCTOR

by Fred Rogers

LANGUAGE CONCEPTS
Exposure – inches, feet, pounds
Mastery – measure, weigh

This book should be shared with children the first month of school as an introduction to the general concepts of measuring and weighing. A scale for weighing and a growth chart for measuring should be an integral part of the room all year long. As the introductory activity, a class bar graph should be used to record each child's weight and height; then this activity should be repeated at regular intervals throughout the year. Initially, children will be expected to grasp an idea of what it means to be measured and weighed and be able to compare who weighs more or less by observing the graph. As the year progresses, many activities with measurement will extend students' concepts, and they will also be able to make their own bar graphs.

THE BIGGEST NOSE

by Kathy Caple

LANGUAGE CONCEPTS

Mastery – bigger, biggest, measured, ruler

Following a general introduction about measuring, children need a variety of activities requiring them to use a ruler and measure small lengths (under 24 inches).

1 ACTIVITY
Measuring "Me"

MATERIALS
- body charts
- yarn
- rulers

Have children complete body charts working in pairs. Use a piece of yarn to match the length of various parts of the body; then hold up to a ruler. *Example: wrist = 4 inches, foot = 8 inches, arm = 12 inches + 5 inches = 17 inches in all.* Cases such as the latter measurement allow practice in "counting on" from 12 up to a maximum of 24.

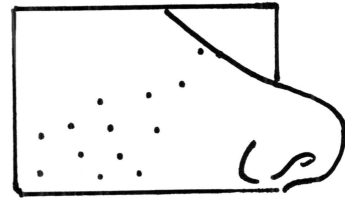

2 ACTIVITY
Comparing Measurements

MATERIALS
- stuffed animals
- "measuring our animals" charts
- large paper for "biggest" chart

Have each child bring a stuffed animal to put in the "measurement corner." Allow children several days to complete their measurements of the animals and record them on their "Measuring Our Animals" chart. Then talk about who has the biggest nose, ears, foot, etc. Children should be able to back up their decisions with facts and in some cases "verify" their decisions by remeasuring in front of the class. Make a class "Biggest" chart identifying the biggest nose, ears, etc.

THE WITCH WHO LIVES DOWN THE HALL

by Donna Guthrie

PREREQUISITES

Children should be able to count by rote to 30 and have a general understanding of the calendar including the concept of a month.

LANGUAGE CONCEPTS

Mastery – fourteenth floor, twenty-five gallon aquarium, one Saturday morning, appeared out of nowhere, only one, table set for two

1 ACTIVITY
Calendar Concepts

MATERIALS

- October calendars
- manipulative cubes
- paper for stories

Use the October calendar to build the concept of "one Saturday morning" and to extend the ordinal numbers concept. Practice placing manipulative cubes on different days in the month extending the use of the ordinal numbers beyond 1-10. Model a story about witches and have them visit various floors in the apartment building on different days during October. The class then places a manipulative cube on the proper date. Allow the children to then take turns creating their own stories about Saturday morning visits to different floors. *Example: On the third Saturday in October the witch visits her ghost friend, who lives on the thirteenth floor. Extend this activity and integrate with writing by having the children write a story about their favorite Halloween characters using the ordinal numbers throughout the story.*

2 ACTIVITY
Witch Problem-Solving

MATERIALS
- mural paper
- paint, markers, or other decorating materials

Make a classroom mural of witches living in an apartment house. Fill the apartment house with their many Halloween friends. When the mural is complete, each child should write one witch problem depicting a scene within the mural. *Example: There are eight witches living on the fourth floor. There are four ghosts living on the same floor. How many more witches live on the fourth floor than ghosts?*

3 ACTIVITY
Double The Witches

MATERIALS
- 20 witch manipulatives per child
- paper for witch booklets

Witches like to travel in groups of the same number. Have the children use 20 witches to practice oral stories using the "doubles." *Example: Five witches made the cats yowl and 5 witches made the dogs yelp. How many witches made the cats and dogs afraid? Then have the children work in pairs to illustrate all the doubles up to 10 + 10 using witch pairs. Write the corresponding number sentence for each illustration and make it into a witch booklet.*

4 ACTIVITY
Beginning Place Value With Witches

MATERIALS

- 19 witch manipulatives
- manipulative cubes
- 10s and 1s recording sheets

The teacher puts any number of witches (11-19) into a paper bag. Each child takes turns drawing the witches from the bag and then counting them by placing a manipulative cube on each witch. Then they pick up one manipulative cube at a time, counting and connecting the cubes until there is a group of ten at which time they call out, "Ten witches!" They continue connecting those over ten and call the remaining number, such as in "six witches." They write the number in expanded notation form as 10 + 6 = 16 (on the chalkboard). Once children are familiar with this procedure, they may use the witch pieces and manipulative cubes on their own, recording their number sentences on a 10s and 1s sheet.

PUMPKIN, PUMPKIN

by Jeannie Titherington

PREREQUISITES

Children should be able to count by rote to 30 and recognize basic shapes.

LANGUAGE CONCEPTS

Mastery – grew, six pumpkin seeds

1 ACTIVITY
Calendar Concepts

MATERIALS

- 1 inch graph paper or calendar outline
- crayons or markers
- manipulative cubes
- ordinal word cards (1-10)

The concepts of time introduced in September can be reviewed and extended in October by the children's calendars. Note the day of the week on which October starts, and mark each day's passing by drawing a jack o' lantern in the appropriate place. Extend counting by rote to 31 as needed, and review ordinal numbers 1-10, this time using word cards.

2 ACTIVITY
Geometric Shapes On Pumpkins

MATERIALS

- flannel board set
- construction paper
- scissors
- paste

Review basic shapes (circle, triangle, square) using flannel board cutouts. Have each child make up a story about Mr. Jack O' Lantern and describe how he looks using the appropriate terms. Children may then construct their own paper jack o' lantern. Note: Use each of the four basic geometric shapes somewhere on your jack o' lantern.

3 ACTIVITY
Ordering Pumpkins

MATERIALS
- variety of different-sized pumpkins
- scale

Bring in a variety of pumpkins. Arrange them in a straight row. Have the children order them in a variety of ways to develop their vocabulary for making distinctions: biggest to smallest, largest to thinnest, tallest to shortest, fattest to thinnest, roughest to smoothest, etc. Using a scale, weigh the pumpkins; then arrange them in a straight row from lightest to heaviest. (Older or more advanced children might record and compare sizes using a bar graph or line graph.)

4 ACTIVITY
Estimating Pumpkin Seeds

MATERIALS
- pumpkin
- estimating jar
- newsprint graph
- variety of small objects

Cut open one pumpkin (smaller pumpkins for younger children, larger pumpkins for older children). Estimate and record on a newsprint graph how many seeds each child guesses are inside the pumpkin. Following this activity, discuss how difficult it is to estimate large numbers. "Many" seeds are harder to guess than "few" seeds. Now count out the seeds in groups of ten and record as such. Find the total seeds and compare with original estimates. As a follow-up to this activity, begin an "estimation jar" activity as a daily activity beginning with a clear jar and a small number of objects needed to fill it (within the group's counting range).

5 ACTIVITY
Roasting Pumpkin Seeds

MATERIALS
- small toaster oven
- pumpkin seeds
- cooking oil
- salt as desired
- recipe for roasting pumpkin seeds

Follow the recipe and cook seeds for $1/2$ to 1 hour. Have children watch the clock and observe how far the clock hands move during cooking.

6 ACTIVITY
Counting Pumpkin Seeds

MATERIALS
- 100 number boards
- pumpkin seeds (dried or roasted)
- large 100 chart for teacher

Extend the pattern learned in counting the thirties to the forties and above. Have each child place a pumpkin seed on top of the number as it is said. Examine patterns within 100: the 10s pattern, the 5s pattern, and the 2s pattern. Use the pumpkin seeds and the 100s board to practice counting by 1s, 2s, 5s, and 10s throughout the month.

7 ACTIVITY
Reverse Counting With Pumpkins

MATERIALS
- flannel board pumpkins
- flannel board
- "Ten Little Indians" song

Practice reverse counting first from 10-1; then extend to 20-1. Practice to the tune of *Ten Little Indians* modifying it as follows: 10 little, 9 little, 8 little pumpkins..., 7 little, 6 little, 5 little pumpkins..., 4 little, 3 little, 2 little pumpkins..., 1 little pumpkin left.

WILLIS

by James Marshall

PREREQUISITES
Children should be able to count by rote to 30 and recognize the following coins: a penny, nickel, and a dime.

LANGUAGE CONCEPTS
Exposure – pay, worth, salary, minute
Mastery – 10 cents, 19 cents, 29 cents, a penny, a ticket

1 ACTIVITY
Dramatizing Willis

MATERIALS
- play or real coins (dimes, nickels, and pennies)
- sunglasses
- paper tickets

After hearing the story of *Willis*, children should recreate the story for their classmates through dramatization. Depending upon their developmental level, in successive dramatizations they may wish to change the price of the sunglasses to another amount between 30 cents and 99 cents. Each time they do this, they may also change the amount Snake has from 10 cents to 50 cents (in amounts of 10). This means that as a group they will need to determine how much more money they will need to buy the sunglasses each time. They also need to decide how many friends come to the talent show each time. This allows natural conversation about mathematics in a real situation.

2 ACTIVITY
Counting Pennies, Nickels, And Dimes

MATERIALS
- toy money (dimes, nickels, and pennies per child)
- 100 number boards for each child

Review counting from 1-100 using the number board. Review counting by 5s by having each child first place a penny on each number on the number board. When each child gets to 5, he/she may then take off the pennies and place a nickel on number 5. Continue with pennies up to 9. Ten will be two 5s or two nickels. Fifteen will be three 5s and so on up to 100 which equals twenty 5s. The same pattern may be followed to review counting by 10s. After nine pennies, pick up the pennies and put a dime on ten. Two 10s equals 20 and so on up to ten 10s equals 100. Conclude by going back and counting by 5s and 10s in a rote fashion. This entire procedure should be repeated for several days until children are comfortable with counting by 5s, 10s, nickels, and dimes.

3 ACTIVITY
Extending Place Value With Willis

MATERIALS
- 10s and 1s recording sheets
- toy coins (9 dimes and pennies)

Children have learned through reading and dramatizing Willis that 10 + 19 = 29, so we can sometimes have more than ten 1s if we do not regroup them into 10s. Discuss this concept thoroughly using dimes and pennies as manipulatives. Now have the children work in pairs to see how many similar number sentences they can form a picture of (using dimes and pennies). They must record on their 10s and 1s sheet where there are more than 10 in the 1s column. (Maximum number = 99.)

SYLVESTER AND THE MAGIC PEBBLE

by William Steig

LANGUAGE CONCEPTS

Exposure – dawn, less than a mile away, night followed day and day followed night over and over again, fall, winter, spring, summer

Mastery – unusual shapes and colors, perfectly round

Review – day before yesterday

1 ACTIVITY
Sorting Pebbles

MATERIALS
- 30 pebble collections brought in by each child
- yarn, hoops, or sorting boards
- materials for making a group graph

Have each child bring in a collection of 30 pebbles. Children should then work in groups of three to four and use the pebbles to practice sorting by a single attribute: color, shape, and size. After each sorting, the children should discuss which pile has more, less, how many more, and how many less. As a culminating activity, groups should make a real graph using the attribute of their choice and the pebble collection of their choice.

2 ACTIVITY
The Magic Pebble Number Sentence

MATERIALS
- children's pebble collection
- red markers
- paper cups

Begin by having each group of children put a certain number of pebbles in a cup (the exact number depends on the fact family to be practiced that day).

Each group then selects a certain number of pebbles to be "magic" and colors those pebbles with a red marker. One by one the groups shake the pebbles out of their cup, make a number sentence depicting their pebbles, and write the appropriate number sentence on the board. This activity may be repeated by making a "different" number of pebbles magic. It may then be extended by changing the number of pebbles in each group's cup and practicing another fact family.

3 ACTIVITY
Sylvester's Season Mobile

MATERIALS
- four 3" x 5" oaktag pieces per child
- crayons or markers
- yarn
- hole punch

Have the children draw pictures of Sylvester, the rock, during each of the four seasons of the year. If these are done on 3" x 5" oaktag, they can easily be made into a mobile using yarn and a hole punch. Each child must put the seasons into the order in which they occur each year. Talk about when Sylvester turned into a rock and when he reappeared within the context of the seasons.

4 ACTIVITY
"Pebble Math" Activities

Use some of the "Pebble Math" activities by William Gibbs (Creative Publications). Activities should be selected which are appropriate to the child's developmental level. This provides a good opportunity to diversify the activities in the class according to ability. These activities both reinforce basic math concepts and encourage problem-solving.

OUR GARAGE SALE

by Anne Rockwell

LANGUAGE CONCEPTS
Exposure – 15 years
Mastery – prices, enough money
Review – pair of boots

1 ACTIVITY
Counting Money

MATERIALS
- play coins (pennies, nickels, dimes, quarters, half dollars)
- "How Much Money" boards
- money pot

To prepare the children for activity 2, review the value of coins (penny, nickel, dime, quarter, and half dollar). Have the children practice counting out money by playing the "How Much Money" game with two teams. Each child gets an individual game board. The pot of money is put in the center of the teams. When it is a child's turn, he/she draws a small card with a coin amount on it. He/she then takes the coins needed, spreads them out on his/her game board, and counts out "how much money." Children may assist the other members of the team. If the money is counted correctly, it may be kept by that team. Otherwise it is put back into the pot. The game continues until all the money in the pot is gone.

2 ACTIVITY
Our Garage Sale

MATERIALS
- garage sale items
- play coins
- price tags

Give the children a few days to bring in some old items from home. Work as a group to label them with realistic prices (1-99 cents). On the day of the garage sale, each child gets to visit the sale. Children may purchase the item(s) of their choice provided they count out the right amount of money for the object.

3 ACTIVITY
Graphing Our Profits

MATERIALS
- paper for estimates
- chart for graph

When all the profits from the garage sale are in, have the class estimate how many pennies, nickels, dimes, etc., were earned. Record the estimates. Then construct a pictograph or bar graph to actually show all the money made at the garage sale. Those children who are capable should be encouraged and assisted in finding the grand profit.

THE TWELVE DAYS OF CHRISTMAS – A CHRISTMAS CAROL

LANGUAGE CONCEPTS
Exposure – ordinal numbers
Mastery – first, twelfth

1 ACTIVITY
Singing *The Twelve Days Of Christmas*

MATERIALS
- individual copies of *The Twelve Days Of Christmas*
- crayons or markers
- signs with the ordinal numbers (1-12)

Give each child a copy of *The Twelve Days Of Christmas* and teach the song to the children with the words in front of them. Have them find and circle each ordinal number with a different-colored marker or crayon. Next give 12 children signs with the ordinal numbers on them. Have them sit on chairs in front of the class. When their number comes along in the story, they should stand up.

2 ACTIVITY
Illustrating *The Twelve Days Of Christmas*

MATERIALS
- 12" x 18" white construction paper or mural paper
- crayons or markers

Give each child a 12" x 18" sheet of white construction paper. Fold it or mark it off so there are 6 rectangles on each side. Label each rectangle "The First Day of Christmas," etc., and draw a picture of the gift for that day. (The ordinal numbers could be put on the board that day in mixed-up order.)

Alternative:
Make a class mural of *The Twelve Days Of Christmas*.

3 ACTIVITY

Dramatizing *The Twelve Days Of Christmas*

MATERIALS
- materials for stick puppets
- long folding table
- flip chart for beginning words of song

Make this delightful song into a puppet show. Have the children make simple stick puppets for each of the gifts. One child might serve as the narrator who stands to the left side using a flip chart with the words "On the First Day of Christmas," etc. Twelve children kneel behind a long folding table and hold up the appropriate puppets as needed. The remaining children stand to the right side and sing the song. Parts may be interchanged frequently so all children get to participate in all parts.

THE SANDMAN

by Rob Shepperson

LANGUAGE CONCEPTS
Exposure – didn't have to wait long, after awhile

Mastery – even after 100, Jay was still counting

Review – every night, one night, late, seconds

1 ACTIVITY
Counting Over 100

MATERIALS
- manipulative cubes or other manipulatives to serve as sheep
- small chalkboards for each group

Working in groups of four, have the children count out 100 sheep. Then have each group see how many more sheep they can count. Continue to use the manipulatives and record their final total on the small chalkboards. Share each group's results with the class as a whole comparing the quantities. Make a class number line on the large chalkboard to see the totals from the least to the greatest.

2 ACTIVITY
"I'm Out" Game

MATERIALS
- game board
- colored counters
- instruction cards

This is a board game to be played with a

maximum of 5 participating children. Children place different-colored counters on the tenth rung. Instruction cards are shuffled and placed down. Children draw the cards and follow the instructions by moving the counter up/down and orally stating the number sentence associated with the move. The game continues until one child successfully climbs back up the mountain with his/her sheep (markers).

3 ACTIVITY
Double The Sheep

MATERIALS
- 10 sheep patterns per child
- 1 gate pattern per child
- cotton balls

Duplicate the sheep pattern and the gate pattern on oaktag for each child. Each child should cut out ten sheep and then paste cotton balls on each sheep if he/she desires. The children will use these sheep manipulatives throughout the month to reinforce the "doubles" addition facts up to ten in conjunction with the recitation of the following poem:

One and one makes two,
One for me and one for you.
Two and two makes four,
Watch the sheep go through the door.
Three and three makes six,
The carpenter will soon fix.
Four and four makes eight,
The door must swing like a gate.
Five and five makes ten,
Slowly the sheep leave their pen.

THE POST OFFICE BOOK

by Gail Gibbons

LANGUAGE CONCEPTS

Mastery – stamps show the cost, heavy costs more than lighter, zip code, divides the oversized or odd-shaped mail from the regular mail

1 ACTIVITY
Classroom Post Office

MATERIALS

- scale or balance scale
- materials for making stamps
- 2 large cardboard boxes
- styrofoam trays
- stamp for cancelling
- large paper for zip code map
- shoe boxes for individual mailboxes

This is a perfect way to integrate the "3 Rs" within the classroom, and the busy Christmas mailing time is most suited to capturing the enthusiasm of the children. Begin by setting up a small post office in the corner of the room. There should be a small scale or balance scale to determine "light or heavy" and thereby the appropriate cost. Various children may be assigned the task of creating stamp designs and identifying their cost. Have two large cardboard boxes to separate oversized or odd-shaped mail from regular mail. Gather materials for cancelling packages. Several children may wish to enlarge the zip code map found in the book and then post the map prominently in the post office. Styrofoam trays will be needed also to be labeled as zip code trays. The final preparation step is for each individual child to make his/her own mailbox to be located at his/her desk.

2 ACTIVITY
Reading Zip Codes

MATERIALS
- zip code map as made in activity 1

Using the large zip code map, practice identifying zip codes depending on the developmental level of the children. Young children may simply read the numbers in the correct order. Older children would benefit by reading them correctly as ten thousands.

3 ACTIVITY
Mailing Letters And Packages

MATERIALS
- materials for letters and cards
- wrapping materials

Practice correctly writing both return addresses and delivery addresses on envelopes and packages. Children may then create their own Christmas cards, Christmas letters, and packages to send one another. Each child should decide on his/her own address including the zip code and have it labeled accurately on his/her individual mailbox. Children will soon realize how important number accuracy is as they attempt to both mail and receive letters and packages!

4 ACTIVITY
Working In The Post Office

MATERIALS
- materials from activity 1
- play money

On a daily basis, several children must be assigned to post office duty. Such duties include:
- weighing incoming mail
- determining the postage cost based on the weight and collecting the correct money
- checking accuracy of addresses
- cancelling the mail
- sorting it into regular vs. oversized containers
- sorting mail into the correct zip code trays

This is valuable practice in determining numbers greater than and less than other five digit numbers. (If this should be determined inappropriate for your level children, simply omit this last step.)

5 ACTIVITY
Delivering Letters And Packages

Several children must serve as daily postal carriers who transfer the mail from the post office to the children's mailboxes. Perhaps this could be done most easily during recess or lunchtime when most children are out of the room. (If all these concurrent activities continue throughout December, they should help children understand how to mail items correctly and how our postal system works.)

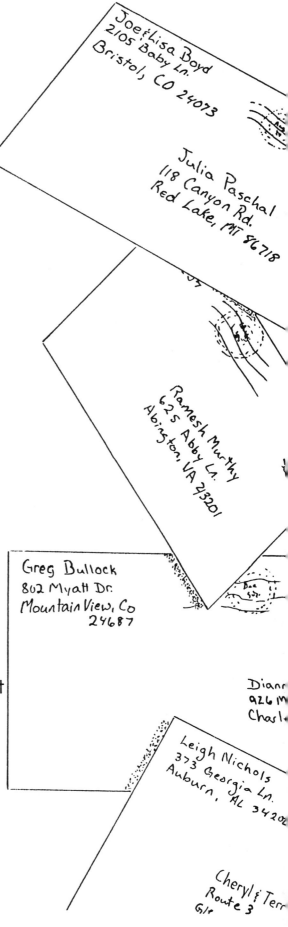

HOW LITTLE PORCUPINE PLAYED CHRISTMAS

by Joseph Slate

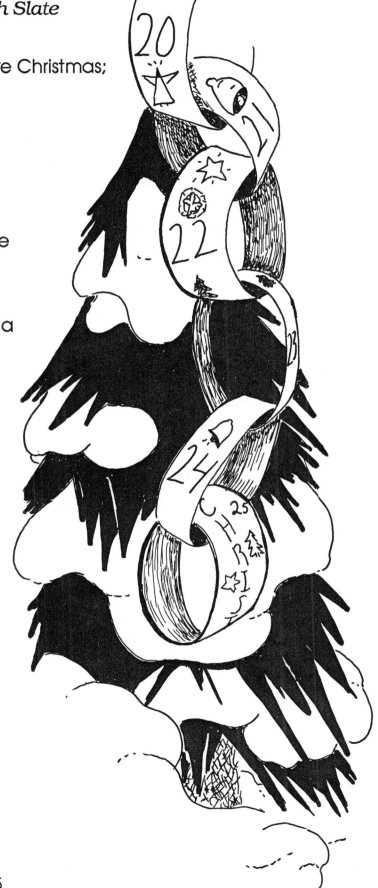

LANGUAGE CONCEPTS

Mastery – four, three, and two days before Christmas; the night before Christmas

1 ACTIVITY
Calendar Concepts

MATERIALS

- 1 inch graph paper or calendar outline
- crayons or markers
- colored paper strips for chains

Use this book in conjunction with making a December calendar and practice identifying "four days before Christmas," etc. Children may also enjoy making a December chain of 25 links for home. One chain must be removed each day until it is "the night before Christmas." Work previously done with ordinal numbers should be reviewed, and the ordinal numbers may be extended if the children are developmentally ready.

2 ACTIVITY
A Doubles Christmas Tree

MATERIALS

- small artificial tree
- styrofoam balls
- toothpicks
- glue
- glitter (for spiny stars)
- tags for "doubles" number sentences

Set up a small pine tree in the math corner and decorate it all over with "spiny stars." Make the spiny stars using the doubles facts learned in the "Double the Sheep" activity on page 31. Extend these facts to include 6 + 6 = 12, 7 + 7 = 14, 8 + 8 =16, 9 + 9 = 18, and 10 + 10 = 20. Put a tag with the appropriate number sentence on each spiny star and leave the sum in the form of a missing number. Once the tree has been completed, the children may use it frequently to practice the doubles in game format. Working in pairs or small groups, the children should begin by removing all the spiny stars. Each child then selects a star and reads the number sentence on its accompanying tag. If he/she can insert the correct missing number, he/she may then put the star anywhere on the tree. The game continues until the tree is fully decorated again.

3 ACTIVITY
Little Porcupine Problems

MATERIALS
- 12" x 18" construction paper for story background sheets
- manipulative cubes or other manipulatives for animals

Have the children analyze the story to discover how many "friends" Little Porcupine has. If there are friends plus Little Porcupine, how many animals are there altogether? This number now becomes the "magic number" for creating story problems in this activity. Each child designs his/her own story background sheet. The teacher models some sample stories; then the children create and share their stories orally. *Example: 1. Fox, Duckling, and Pig do not want Little Porcupine to be the Wiseman. How many would like him to be the Wiseman? 2. Everyone but Mouse tells Little Porcupine to be the clean-up person. How many want Little Porcupine to be the clean-up person?*

JANUARY BRINGS THE SNOW

by Sara Coleridge

LANGUAGE CONCEPTS
Exposure – names of the months
Mastery – brings

1 ACTIVITY
Calendar Concepts

MATERIALS
- 1 inch graph paper or calendar outline
- crayons or markers
- chart for class graph

Begin the new year by an intensive look at a new calendar. Compare last year's calendar with the new year's. Point out the year's dates now have different days. What might next year be? Next analyze the meaning of a year in months. Follow up this discussion with reading *January Brings The Snow* and further discussing the weather and characteristics of each month. Make a class graph of the children's birthdays by month. Each child should make an individual January calendar which will be used again in the next activity.

2 ACTIVITY
Something Little In Math

MATERIALS
- January calendars as in activity 1
- small pieces of paper

Have each child think of "something little in math" which may be done as a class activity at the beginning of each day in January. Possible activities might include: counting to 100,

37

reciting all the "doubles," singing a days of the week song or months of the year song, measuring the teacher's cactus plant, counting all the buttons in the classroom, estimating and comparing the number of children buying cafeteria lunches, etc. Each child writes his/her idea on a small piece of paper and puts them into a box. As each activity is drawn from the box, the activities are recorded by the children on their individual calendars on the corresponding date. Calendars are then referred to each morning for the respective activity.

3 ACTIVITY
Poster Of The Year

MATERIALS
- 12" x 18" white construction paper
- coloring materials

Direct the children to make a poster of the year. Divide the large construction paper into 12 parts and label each part with the name of a month. The months should be in sequential order. Draw a picture of what the child likes to do best during each month. Share the posters in small groups; then compare the activities enjoyed. *Example (questions for discussion): How many children like to swim? (Record the number on the board for all to see.); How many children like to go camping; How many more children like to swim than camp; How many children like to both swim and camp?*

TIME

by Henry Pluckrose

LANGUAGE CONCEPTS

Mastery – measure time, big hand, little hand, clocks, watches, seconds, minutes, hours, midnight, midday, days of the week, week, month, year

1 ACTIVITY
Time During The Day

MATERIALS

- large demonstration clock
- small individual clocks for the children

This book may serve as an excellent introduction to time. It makes clear the functions of both hands on the clock and relates various times within a normal day. As the teacher reads the book, he/she should allow the children to explore the measurement of time as suggested by the various activities in the book. *Example: How many times can you clap in a second? How many letters of the alphabet can you write in 10 seconds or 60 seconds? How long does it take to have breakfast, lunch, and dinner?* Following the reading of the book, give each child a small individual clock. Allow five minutes for free exploration. Briefly demonstrate time on the hour. Then model the creation of story problems about the children in the class. *Example: Today is Saturday and Mary is glad she doesn't have to get up so early in the morning. What does Mary's clock look like when she gets up on Saturday? Emphasize that there is more than one appropriate answer. Once children have shown some understanding of time on the hour, allow them to join in creating some story problems.*

2 ACTIVITY
My Time Book

MATERIALS
- construction paper
- newsprint for booklets
- markers
- crayons
- other writing materials
- blank clockfaces or a clock stamp

Have each child make an individual booklet showing a normal day in his/her life. Each page should contain a clockface depicting the time, an appropriate illustration, and a sentence describing the activity and when it took place. *Example: I leave for school at 8 o'clock.* Limit the times to hourly ones as appropriate to the children's developmental level. Each page in the booklet should be in sequential order throughout the day.

3 ACTIVITY
Using A Stopwatch

MATERIALS
- stopwatch
- chart for graph

The Stopwatch by D. Lloyd and P. Dale may be used to extend the understanding of time for both seconds and minutes. After reading *The Stopwatch* to the class, allow them to explore and use a stopwatch. Time some simple activities such as hopping 10 times, singing a song, etc. For one day, use the stopwatch to time various classroom activities. Record the activities on a graph and compare the times to determine the longest activity, the shortest, activities which take the same amount of time, etc.

CURIOUS GEORGE

by H. A. Rey

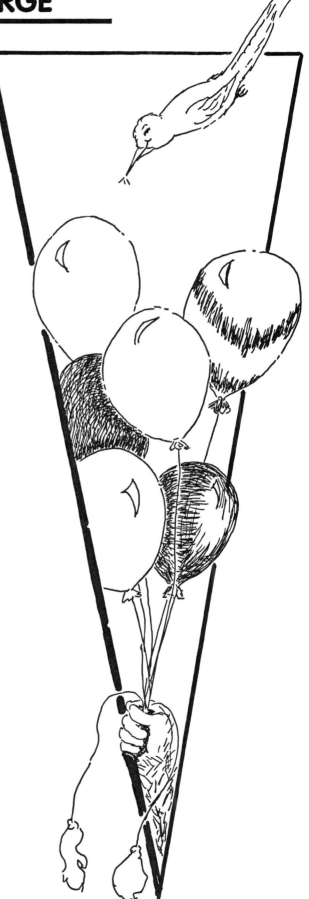

LANGUAGE CONCEPTS
Mastery – bought, broke loose, all the balloons

Balloon Stories

MATERIALS
- Curious George mats
- balloon manipulatives

Have the children work in pairs using the Curious George mats and the balloon manipulatives. They may create their own stories about buying balloons, balloons breaking loose, balloons bursting, balloons floating, etc. As one child creates the story, his/her partner should write an accompanying number sentence and solve the story.
Example: Curious George was floating above the park with eight balloons. Suddenly a bird flew by and burst two balloons with his beak. How many balloons are there now? ($8 - 2 = 6$; 6 balloons left)

2 ACTIVITY
Comparing Numbers To 100

MATERIALS
- balloon work sheet
- two dice for each pair of students

Let children work in pairs. Each pair has two dice, and each child has an individual balloon work sheet. Each child in the pair rolls a two digit number and names his/her number. Whenever possible, each child must then create a "different" number sentence to compare the two digit numbers rolled.

Example: 76 is greater than 43, 43 is less than 76. Each child records his/her number sentence on any balloon on his/her work sheet. The game continues until all the balloons have a number sentence in them. At this point, each child rolls one last two digit number. The child with the highest number "directs" how his/her partner and he/she shall color his/her balloons.

Example: multicolored, all blue, all striped, so many striped and so many solid green, etc.

3 ACTIVITY
Reverse Counting Balloons

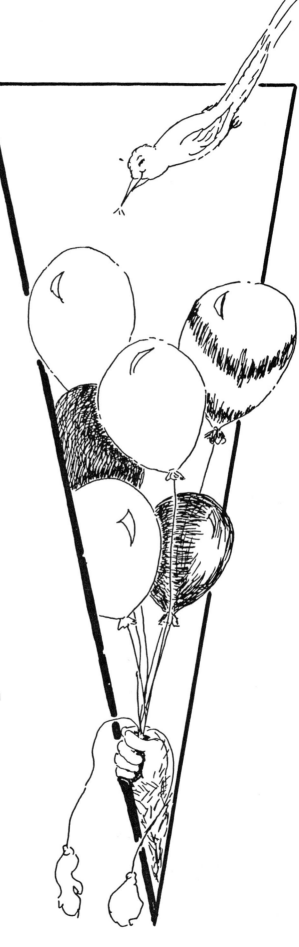

MATERIALS
- balloon work sheet
- balloon manipulatives

Working with their partners, children should place the colored balloon manipulatives on their balloon work sheet counting in order orally. They then reverse the procedure and remove them one at a time using reverse counting. After practicing this until proficient, each child should write the numbers from 20-0 on his/her balloon work sheet in reverse order. When his/her partner has verified that the numbers are written correctly, he/she may then color his/her work sheet.

4 ACTIVITY
Balloon Sale

MATERIALS

- large bag of balloons
- small number tags (1-10) in a paper cup
- play money

Have a class balloon sale! Each child should receive a turn to be the balloon vendor and sell the balloons for 2, 5, or 10 cents each. Put small number tags (1-10) in a cup. Each customer draws a number tag to determine how many balloons he/she will buy. The vendor must figure out the total cost. This will reinforce the previous work done on adding groups of 2, 5, and 10. The customer must then count out the correct money for his/her balloon purchase.

5 ACTIVITY
Estimating Balloons

MATERIALS

- large glass jar
- assorted balloons
- estimating box
- chart for graph

Fill the class estimation jar with assorted balloons for this week. Each day the children may either revise or keep their original estimate and put it in the estimating box. On Friday, make a class graph depicting the estimates and discuss in detail. Count the balloons by grouping them into 10s and 1s. Talk about strategies for estimating and ways to improve in estimating.

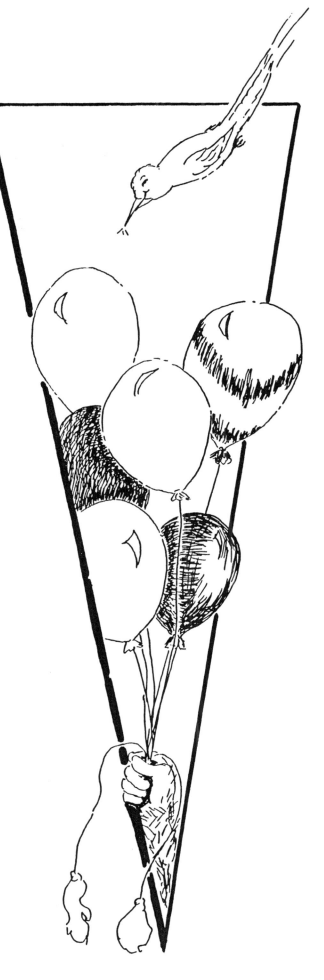

LION DANCER – ERNIE WAN'S CHINESE NEW YEAR

by Kate Waters and Madeline Slovenz-Low

LANGUAGE CONCEPTS

Mastery – most important day, every day, thousands of visitors, new year, midnight, early the next morning, 2,637 years older, every twelve years

A Chinese Horoscope

MATERIALS
- copy of Chinese horoscope (per child)
- crayons or markers

Have the children bring in the complete birthdates of five people of different ages. *Example: Brothers, sisters, parents, grandparents, neighbors, etc. Match the year of their birth with the year on the Chinese horoscope. Circle all five dates using crayons or markers. Pick one date to write about the personality traits of the person in comparison with the horoscope.*

How Much Money?

MATERIALS
- play money
- red and gold wrapping paper
- index cards
- construction paper for posters
- grab bag

Using play money, each child wraps an amount from 10-99 cents in small red and gold packages and places them in the grab bag. He/she then writes the amount on an index card and pins it on the bulletin board entitled, "How Much Money?" When all the coin packages are ready, each child draws out a package, counts the coins, and finds the matching amount on the bulletin board. The culminating activity is the child's poster depicting how he/she will spend his/her money during the Chinese holiday. Note: In dividing the money between several items, the **total** must be what was received in the red or gold package.

3 ACTIVITY
A Money Tree

MATERIALS
- large pine branches in a vase
- unlined index cards
- play coins
- clear tape
- calculators

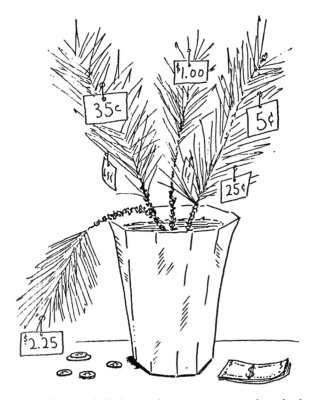

Place some large pine branches in a vase to make a money tree just as the Chinese do. Have each child draw a money amount from a small box. The child must count out that amount of money and then make a money card to decorate the tree. The total money on the card should be highlighted. To discover how much money total is on the class tree, teach the children to use a calculator as an option to add large amounts. They should be encouraged to practice doing so on their own until they attain the correct sum.

4 ACTIVITY
Glass Bead Patterns

MATERIALS
- plastic or glass beads
- index cards for pattern cards
- string

During the Chinese Lantern Festival, doorways are decorated with glass beads. Obtain a large amount of plastic or glass beads for the children to string making their own pattern. Each child should then make a pattern card labeling his/her pattern. *Example: Joan's pattern – ABBACAD. These pattern cards then may be used as task cards for the rest of the class to replicate during free time.*

THE BOY WHO HATED VALENTINE'S DAY

by Sally Wittman

LANGUAGE CONCEPTS

Exposure – 40 valentines so everyone gave
Mastery – didn't receive a single valentine,
nothing, spring, summer, fall, winter,
20 valentines for himself

Twenty Valentines

MATERIALS

- 1 show box per child
- valentine pattern
- assorted construction paper for valentines
- paper for recording number sentences

Each child should decorate a shoe box as
his/her valentine manipulative box and then
should make 20 valentines to keep inside
and use as manipulatives. Arrange the
children in groups of four and pose this
problem. You have 20 valentines to distribute
among the three friends in your group.
Discover how many different ways you can
distribute them if you never give more than 9
to any one friend. *Example: 9 + 5 + 6 = 20, 8
+ 4 + 8 = 20, etc. Keep a group list of all the
number sentences you can make. At the
end of the activity, share and compare the
results from each group. Discuss how each
number sentence may be written
horizontally as well as vertically. Do the
answers stay the same?*

2 ACTIVITY
Candy Hearts In Doubles

MATERIALS
- candy hearts in bags
- large oaktag – 1 per group
- glue

Give each group of four children a bag of candy hearts, a large piece of oaktag, and some glue. Each group should make a valentine doubles poster beginning with 1 heart + 1 heart = 2 hearts. They should continue until they reach the 40 hearts that Henry received. Discuss the doubles in detail. *Example: What patterns do you see? How many people gave Henry valentines? How many did Henry think each person gave him? Why?*

3 ACTIVITY
Counting Over 100

MATERIALS
- valentine box and valentine manipulatives from activity 1

Discover how many valentines there are total if everyone has 20 in their box. Have the children line up in a horizontal line in front of the room, five at a time. Each child should count his/her valentines "counting on" from the previous child. As they count them slowly, the teacher records the numbers on the board using a 100 board pattern. After counting, analyze the patterns in the numbers on the board. *Example: How are the numbers the same? How are they different? What would the numbers look like if the "grand total" was greater than 400?* Follow up this activity with several opportunities for the children to count beyond 100 using blank 100 board grids.

How Many Hearts?

MATERIALS
- 10" x 10" grids (1" graph paper)
- heart stickers or small paper hearts
- glue

Have the children work in pairs, and give each pair some grids and a cup of hearts (a number between 100-500). One child pastes the hearts on the grid, counting them outloud. The partner writes the corresponding numbers below the hearts until all the hearts have been counted. When all the groups have completed the activity, have the pairs report to the entire group on their findings. Display the heart grids around the room.

Hearts In 10s And 1s

MATERIALS
- candy hearts
- paper cups
- 10s and 1s recording sheets

Have the children work in groups of three. Give each group a bag of candy hearts, an empty cup, and a 10s and 1s recording sheet. The first member of the group randomly places an amount of hearts into the empty cup. The second member shakes the hearts out and arranges them in groups of 10 with 1s left over. The third member records the number found. *Example: 30 hearts + 5 hearts = 35 hearts.*

LITTLE RABBIT'S LOOSE TOOTH

by Lucy Bate

LANGUAGE CONCEPTS

Mastery – loose, lose, not a lot of money, worth more
Review – first, names of the days of the week,
penny, dime

1 ACTIVITY
Mr. Smile Stories

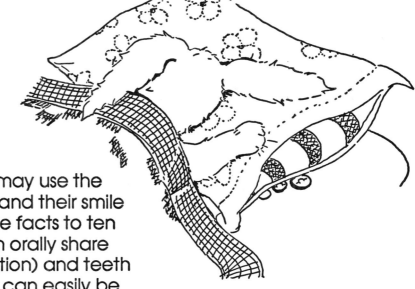

MATERIALS
- bean counters
- smile boards

Working in small groups, children may use the
white side of their bean counters and their smile
boards to review and reinforce the facts to ten
within a story situation. Have them orally share
stories about "lost" teeth (subtraction) and teeth
"growing in" (addition). The book can easily be
integrated with a health/science unit and the
concept that the children have ten primary
teeth on the bottom.

2 ACTIVITY
Flannel Board Teeth

MATERIALS
- flannel board
- 20 flannel teeth
- recording sheets for number sentences

This activity allows extension of the concept of ten primary teeth on the bottom
to include ten primary teeth on the top for a total of 20 primary teeth. The
teacher may begin by reviewing the doubles to twenty as he/she places the
"full mouth" on the flannel board. The teacher should then model a variety of
stories about teeth to reinforce the basic number facts to twenty. As this is
done, the children will record the corresponding number sentence on their
recording sheets. The children should then create their own stories for the class.
Then later students can expound on them as a follow-up activity.

3 ACTIVITY
What Did Little Rabbit Eat?

MATERIALS
- construction paper for posters

Review the days of the week by having each child create a poster depicting Little Rabbit's menu. What days are missing? Now that Little Rabbit lost her loose tooth, what might she eat on those remaining days?

4 ACTIVITY
Our Lost Teeth

MATERIALS
- chart for lost teeth graph
- estimate chart

Conduct a class discussion on teeth that have been lost by the students. Have each child estimate how many teeth he/she thinks he/she will lose the rest of the year, and record his/her estimates on a chart. Make a class graph to record lost teeth for the remainder of the year. Refer to both charts throughout the year on a regular basis.

5 ACTIVITY
The Tooth Fairy Game

MATERIALS
- envelope with a lost tooth
- play coins

Select one child to be Little Rabbit. Let him/her pretend to go to sleep with his/her lost tooth in an envelope. Select another child to be the Tooth Fairy who replaces the lost tooth with a certain amount of money (10-99 cents). When Little Rabbit awakes, he/she counts how much money he/she has received. The rest of the class must now try to guess the correct amount to become the next Little Rabbit. Little Rabbit may assist the class in their guesses by giving clues such as more, less, 10 cents more, double that amount, etc. The new Little Rabbit also gets to select the new Tooth Fairy.

GET READY FOR ROBOTS

by Patricia Lauber

LANGUAGE CONCEPTS

Mastery – squares, circles, other shapes, map, instructions, measured

ACTIVITY
Collecting, Sorting, And Classifying

MATERIALS
- assortment of robot materials collected
- trays for sorting

Have the children bring in an assortment of nuts, bolts, egg cartons, paper cups, boxes, etc. – any materials that they can imagine using to construct a robot. Once the materials have been brought in, they provide the ideal momentum for some sorting and classifying activities. *Example: Sort all the nuts by color, then shape, then size. How many other ways can nuts be classified?*

ACTIVITY
Creating A Robot

MATERIALS
- paper for robot designs
- assorted materials collected in activity 1
- craft glue

This is a three-step activity which may require several days. Step 1 requires each child to design his/her robot on paper. In addition to the illustration, the children must include an enumerated list of materials and a numerical name for their robot that has some meaning when related to their design.

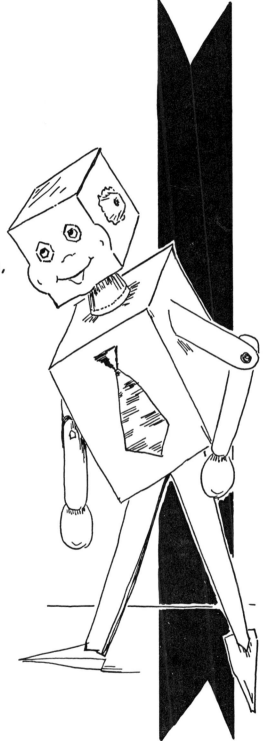

The children should be encouraged to be imaginative and complex. Step 2 is building their robots following their designs. Step 3 lets the children compare their robots to the original design and materials list. Any additions or changes may be made at this time.

3 ACTIVITY
Robot Show

MATERIALS
- assorted paper
- oaktag
- markers
- crayons

Let the children share and discuss their creations with an audience – another class, the school, parents, etc. To make it truly the children's show, they should make their own advertisements, invitations, arrange the display, and decide the format for the show. (This will require several days.)

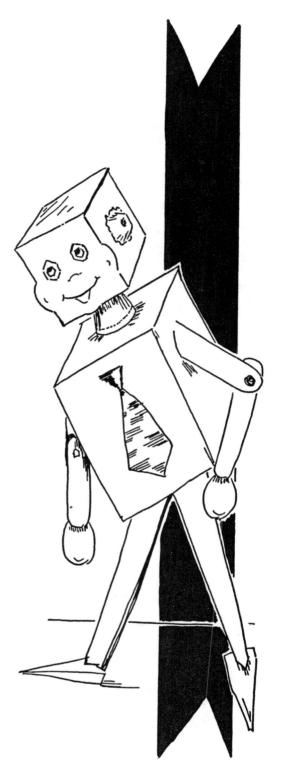

TEDDY BEARS CURE A COLD

by Susanna Gretz

LANGUAGE CONCEPTS
Exposure – few days
Mastery – thermometer, temperature

1 ACTIVITY
Temperature On Thermometers

MATERIALS
- large demonstration thermometer
- charts for graphs

Integrate this story with a science unit on temperature. Use a large demonstration thermometer to talk about its function and the difference between outdoor, indoor, and medical thermometers. Make two class graphs, and record the inside and outside temperatures for a week or more. If you are able to obtain enough medical thermometers for the entire class, it would be good to keep a record of individual body temperatures. Discuss the results of all these in detail.

2 ACTIVITY
Teddy Bear Tales

MATERIALS
- story paper
- book binding

Now that the children have some understanding of temperature, have them create a teddy bear tale about a sick teddy bear.
Note: Use as many math words as possible in your story. Be sure to talk about times and temperatures. Bind the completed tales together to make a class book.

3 ACTIVITY
Teddy Bears In Cages

MATERIALS
- teddy bear counters
- plastic cherry tomato crates/berry baskets
- 10s and 1s recording sheets

Further develop the children's understanding of place value, expanded notation, and regrouping of 10s using teddy bear counters and tomato crates as "cages." Children may work in groups of four, and each group should be given a cage with a random number of bears (any two-digit number to 99) and a recording sheet. Each group should see how many different ways the bears can be rearranged, always keeping them in groups of 10s and 1s. The results are recorded as follows:
48 = 40 + 8, 30 + 18, 20 + 28, 10 + 38. Groups may then exchange bear cages and continue in the same manner.

4 ACTIVITY
Teddy Bear Estimation

MATERIALS
- teddy bear counters
- yarn for different-sized circles
- small chalkboards for recording

Give each group of children assorted yarn lengths for different-sized circles and a box of teddy bear counters. The group must make an estimate as to how many bears it will take to fill up each circle and record the estimates. After each estimation, fill the circle with the teddy bear counters, count, and record. Encourage the groups to experiment with better ways of estimating. When all the groups have finished, make a class list of successful ways to estimate teddy bears.

A BIRTHDAY FOR FRANCES

by Russell Hoban

LANGUAGE CONCEPTS

Exposure – 50 cents, a minute
Mastery – the day before Gloria's birthday, one birthday every year, two months from now, two weeks, half of one
Review – a nickel and two pennies and another nickel and two pennies

A Birthday Drama

MATERIALS
- story props
- calendar of the year

Have the children reenact the story of *A Birthday for Frances*. Prior to the dramatization, use a calendar to discuss an imaginary date for Gloria's birthday, today's date, two months from now (which will be Frances' birthday), and the two weeks Frances will visit Alice. Then have each child mark his/her birthday on the calendar.

Birthday Candles On A Cake

MATERIALS
- birthday cake mat
- birthday candles
- birthday recording sheet

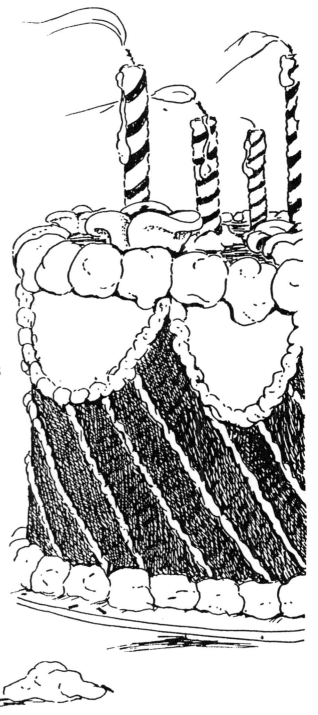

Provide each pair with a birthday cake mat and a box of birthday candles. The first child puts a selected number of candles on the cake and then sings to his/her partner, "How old are you now?" The partner responds and then removes a certain number of candles singing, "How many did I blow out?" Together the pair records a number sentence describing their actions on the birthday recording sheet. *Example: 12 - 6 = 6.*

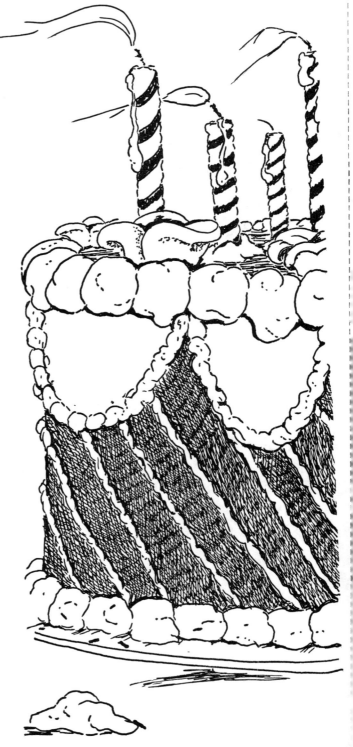

3 ACTIVITY
Sharing With Your Sister

MATERIALS
- flannel board
- fraction pieces (including simulated chocolate bars) for flannel board

The concept of Frances and Gloria each having a "half" of the Chompo bar is a good introduction to fractions. Demonstrate on the flannel board using the chocolate bar flannel pieces. Then extend the fraction concepts to 1/3 and 1/4 by creating fraction stories about Ollie Orange and Brenda Blueberry Bar. Encourage the children to take turns creating their own stories using the demonstration pieces.

4 ACTIVITY
My Own Sharing Story

MATERIALS
- story paper
- construction paper or oaktag
- flannel backing

Have each child write a story about him/her sharing a food item with some friends (maximum of 3). Use appropriate fraction numbers in the story. The children may then draw and cut out the fraction pieces for their story. Emphasize that the fraction parts must be equal size. When the children have put flannel backing on them, they may then share their fraction story with the class demonstrating it on the flannel board.

THE BERENSTAIN BEARS' TROUBLE WITH MONEY

by Stan & Jan Berenstain

LANGUAGE CONCEPTS

Mastery – allowance, made of money, earning money, saving for a rainy day, misers, nest eggs

1 ACTIVITY
Figures Of Speech

MATERIALS
- 12" x 18" construction paper
- markers or crayons

Have the children pick one of the above figures of speech (or do all four) and draw an illustration of what it would look like were it **not** a figure of speech. Share the drawings as a class and discuss the real meanings of the figures of speech.

2 ACTIVITY
Earning Money

MATERIALS
- poster board
- markers
- play money

As a class, decide on an appropriate monetary value for various classroom jobs. Make a poster listing jobs and payments. Have the children take turns being the employer who pays all the employees at the end of each day, accurately counting out their pay. Continue the activity until each child has a turn as the employer.

3 ACTIVITY
What Should I Do With My Allowance?

MATERIALS
- play money
- small pieces of paper
- hat
- writing paper for stories

Put a variety of monetary amounts appropriate to the child's developmental level on small pieces of paper. Have each child draw one out of a hat. This will be the child's allowance for the week. He/she should write a brief story describing what he/she will do with this week's allowance. The allowance may be broken up to buy as many items as desired, but they must total the original amount. Encourage the children to use play money to help them divide it accurately. The teacher should review the various ways to write monetary amounts correctly before the children write their stories.

4 ACTIVITY
Piggy Bank Game

MATERIALS
- large piggy bank
- play coins
- scrap paper for each group

Place a large piggy bank in the center of the room. Divide the children into small groups and give each group a variety of coins and scrap paper. A spokesperson for each group will take turns going to the piggy bank and dropping up to five coins in, naming them as he/she drops them in. *Example: 1 dime, a nickel, 2 pennies, and 1 quarter. He/she then asks, "How much is in the piggy bank?" Each group works together to determine the correct amount with the manipulatives. The first group to accurately name the amount receives the money. The game continues with a new spokesperson for each group.*

5 ACTIVITY
Create A Business

MATERIALS

- assorted materials to make the business "product"
- poster boards
- price tags
- markers
- crayons
- pens
- play money

Let the children discuss a possible class "business" which they can begin. The products sold must be easy to make using materials brought from home and/or available within the classroom. Products then should be priced and sold either within the classroom or to other classrooms in the school, as appropriate. Children should do their own advertising and selling. Customers may make purchases using play money. Objectives are: 1) additional practice counting money and making change, and 2) the opportunity to analyze the best way to "total" the day's profits.

THE LITTLEST DINOSAURS

by Bernard Most

LANGUAGE CONCEPTS

Exposure – over 100 million years

Mastery – feet, inches, about the size of ___

Review – biggest, bigger, littlest, weighed, one half

1 ACTIVITY
How Big Were The Biggest Dinosaurs?

MATERIALS
- tape measure
- estimating chart
- paper for lists
- markers

Extend the children's ability to measure and estimate to include feet as well as inches. Review the use of rulers and the concept that 12 inches equals 1 foot. Make a class estimating chart for the three largest dinosaurs. Now read the first two pages of the book. Then take the class outside to the playground and measure 100 feet, 90 feet, and 75 feet – the measurements of ultrasaurus, brachiosaurus, and brontosaurus. Follow up this activity with small groups of children making lists entitled, "An ultrasaurus is about the size of_____." Share the lists as a class when they are completed.

2 ACTIVITY
How Little Was The Littlest Dinosaur?

MATERIALS
- large bulletin board paper
- poster paint
- rulers and/or tape measure

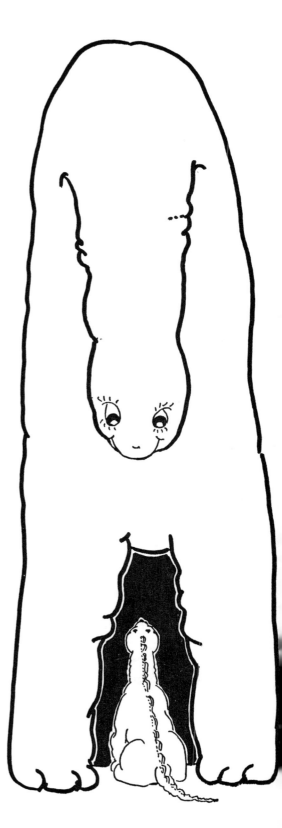

Finish reading *The Littlest Dinosaurs*. Make a class mural depicting the ten littlest dinosaurs. Have the children work in pairs and check the accuracy of the dinosaurs' size. Let the children write individual stories about one of the ten littlest dinosaurs and a problem it had because of its small size.

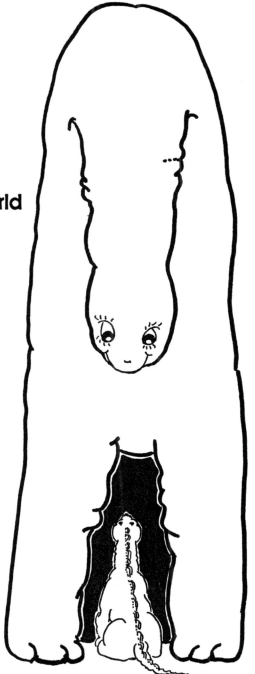

3 ACTIVITY

Comparing The Littlest Dinosaurs To The World

MATERIALS
- rulers
- large chart paper
- markers
- dinosaur work sheets

Divide the class into small groups and provide each group with large chart paper, markers, and rulers. Each group should list the ten littlest dinosaurs and their size and then complete the chart with as many items as they can find that match their sizes. They may begin by measuring items in the classroom. The activity can be continued as a home activity using the dinosaur work sheets and later transferred to the group charts. When the activity is completed, discuss the results as a class and then display the charts in a prominent place within the school for the entire student body to enjoy.

A DROP OF BLOOD

by Paul Showers

LANGUAGE CONCEPTS

Exposure – thousands, millions
Mastery – pints, quarts
Review – hundreds, a single drop of blood,
round and flat, thin in the middle, thick around
the edge, minute, weighs, pounds, half

1 ACTIVITY
Blood In Our Bodies

MATERIALS

- pint and quart containers (transparent)
- water
- labels
- large bulletin board paper
- marker

Conduct a discussion about the difference in
size between a person that weighs 24 pounds,
85 pounds, and 180 pounds. Try to find three
people that match these descriptions with
which the entire class would be familiar. Write
the three names on name tags and divide the
class into three groups. Each group should
receive a name tag and 1) draw a life-size
model of that person, and 2) fill the
appropriate number of containers with the
"blood" of that person (in both pints and
quarts). When each group is finished, place the
models and their "blood" in a central display
position and discuss the results.

2 ACTIVITY
How Much Is A Thousand?

MATERIALS
- 10 cups
- chalkboard

Initiate a class discussion on how much is a "thousand" cells in a single drop of blood. Decide as a class a small, easily collectible item which children may bring in to determine how much is a thousand. Write the number "1,000" on the board and record each 100 items as they are collected. Have the students add the 100s collected until the grand total of 1,000 is reached. Encourage the children to make predictions and revise them during the entire process.

3 ACTIVITY
Exploring Numbers Beyond A Thousand

MATERIALS
- any materials needed for individual projects
- large number signs
- markers

Following the children's understanding of a thousand, encourage them to explore large numbers beyond a thousand. Read *How Much is a Million?* to the class. Those children who desire may choose a number between 1,000 and 10,000 and create an individual project to explain the concept of that number in the Schwartz format. *Example: If you want to count to 2,000, it will take you about _____ minutes. If you can count to 100 in 2 minutes, then you can count to 1,000 in 20 minutes; therefore, it would take about 40 minutes to count to 2,000.*

THE GROUCHY LADYBUG

by Eric Carle

LANGUAGE CONCEPTS

Mastery – at twelve noon, —— - thirty,
quarter to ___, still some aphids left, all the
aphids were gone
Review – at ___ o'clock in the morning, night

1 ACTIVITY
Grouchy Ladybug Time

MATERIALS

- demonstration clocks
- clock stamp
- 12" x 18" drawing paper
- markers or crayons

Provide a small demonstration clock for each
child. As you reread the story of the grouchy
ladybug, have the children depict each time
on their own clock. The beginning of the story
serves as an excellent review of time on the
hour whereas the end of the book may serve
as a good introduction to time on the half and
quarter hour. Upon completing the story, have
the class problem-solve to figure out how many
hours it took the grouchy ladybug to arrive right
back where she started from. Follow up this
lesson by having each child create his/her own
story about any animal and its activities
throughout the day. Use a clock stamp to affix
the time for each event.

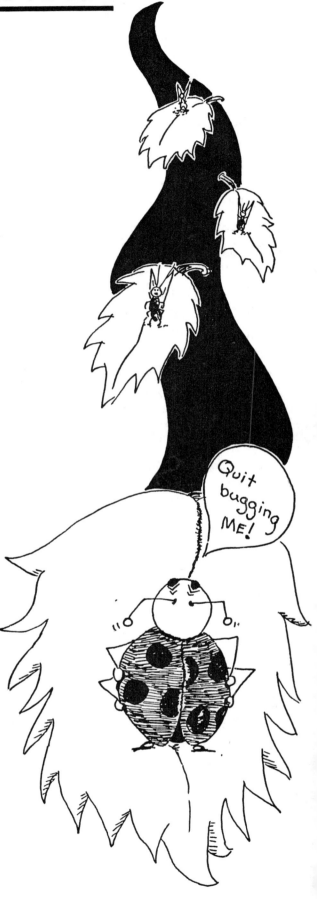

Quit bugging ME!

2 ACTIVITY
Ladybug And Aphid Tales

MATERIALS
- leaf mats
- red bean counters for ladybugs
- black counters/buttons for aphids
- large recording sheets
- markers

Reinforce the basic addition and subtraction facts to 18 by having the class work in small groups and create story problems about the ladybugs and the aphids. Model some sample stories first using the language terms of "many," "left," "gone," etc. Within a group, each child shares a story, and the other children make a picture of the story using their leaf mats and insect manipulatives. One child serves as the teacher's assistant and records the corresponding number sentences on a large recording sheet. At the end of the activity, the assistants report back to the class with all the number sentences enacted by their group.

3 ACTIVITY
Tree Of Symmetry

MATERIALS
- leaf mats
- drawing paper
- markers or crayons

Use the leaf mats to introduce the concept of symmetry (same size and shape) to the class. Then integrate this lesson with a science lesson on common trees and how to recognize them by their unique leaf shapes. Have each child make a pair of symmetric leaves and display them on a class "tree of symmetry."

A BARGAIN FOR FRANCES

by Russell Hoban

LANGUAGE CONCEPTS
Mastery – a bargain, saving all my allowance, dollars, a lot of money, "halfsies" on the dime
Review – cents, spent the rest

1 ACTIVITY
Dramatizing A Bargain For Frances

MATERIALS
- play money (dollars and cents)
- plastic tea set
- china tea set

A reenactment of this story provides good practice in money exchange as well as reinforcing the language concepts within the story. The story may be repeated several times by various groups of students using different amounts of money. Discussion on changing the amounts will help strengthen the concept of "a lot" of money, "halfsies" on the dime, and saving all their allowance.

2 ACTIVITY
"Halfsies" With Money

MATERIALS
- play money
- flannel board
- fraction pieces for the flannel board
- recording paper

Divide the class into groups of four, and provide each group with a variety of coins as well as recording paper. Review the concept of one-half as introduced in the unit on "A Birthday for

Frances." Extend the concept of one-half to money by having each group find the two coins which Frances would use to go halves with a dime. Continue by having each group problem-solve to discover how many other money combinations of halves and their equal amounts can be found. Record these discoveries and later share them with the entire class.

3 ACTIVITY
Bargain Store

MATERIALS
- empty grocery containers
- labels for prices
- markers or crayons
- oaktag for signs
- play money

Create a small supermarket in the classroom. Allow several weeks for the children to bring assorted grocery containers from home. As each child brings them in, he/she may price them individually and arrange them on the store shelves. On a designated day, have the children work in pairs to make a variety of bargain signs. *Example: Corn – 2 cans for 50 cents. The pair must coordinate their bargain with the actual prices so they make sense. Allow the pairs of children to make purchases from the supermarket and work in the store at appropriate times in the day for a period of time. The customer should make only one purchase at a time and must pay for it with the exact amount. The storekeeper must verify that the correct amount of money has been received.*

MAKE WAY FOR DUCKLINGS

by Robert McCloskey

LANGUAGE CONCEPTS
Mastery – in a line
Review – first, all, all day, night

ACTIVITY
Ducks In A Line

MATERIALS
- flannel board
- flannel ducks
- ordinal number cards
- teddy bear counters (1 box per group)

Retell the story using the flannel board and emphasizing that Mrs. Mallard taught the ducklings to walk in a line. Review the concept of ordinal numbers and have the children match the ordinal number cards to the appropriate duck in line. Continue the discussion by asking other ways the ducks might walk in line. As a child suggests pairs of ducks, review counting by 2s. Follow up this activity by having the children work in groups of four with 50 teddy bear counters. Have them arrange the bears in pairs and introduce the concept of even numbers as paired numbers. Now have them arrange the bears when they are not paired but have an odd member. These are the odd numbers.

2 ACTIVITY
Peanuts And Other Nuts

MATERIALS
- assorted nuts (1 can per group)
- classification cards
- large poster boards (1 per group)
- gluesticks

Have the children work in small groups sorting and classifying the nuts in as many possible ways as they can. As one child arranges a set on the classification board, he/she then asks the remaining members of the group to describe the classification he/she has made in a sentence. Complete the group session by making a real graph using all the nuts given to the group. Each group is also responsible for deciding on five questions concerning the graph which will be used in a whole class session the following day.

3 ACTIVITY
Exciting Egg Stories

MATERIALS
- 1 basket per group
- plastic eggs for each basket
- recording paper

This is a good book to integrate with a unit on spring and the birth of new animals. Model some story problems for the children concerning eggs being hatched and those left unhatched, or eggs laid one day and more eggs laid the next day, etc. Divide the children into small groups and have them create their own stories one at a time. The other group members should record the appropriate number sentence and solve for the answer.

ALICE'S ADVENTURES IN WONDERLAND

LANGUAGE CONCEPTS

Mastery – "I'm late for an important date."

Review – night

1 ACTIVITY
White Rabbit Is Late For An Important Date

MATERIALS

- large demonstration clock
- writing paper
- markers or crayons

Read the beginning part of *Alice in Wonderland* stopping when the White Rabbit disappears through the woods again. Integrate math and writing by having the children imagine what White Rabbit's important date might be and the time for his date. Have the children write and illustrate a story describing White Rabbit's important date. Let them include the time he was supposed to be there as well as any other times that indicate how late he really is. Model a possible story for them, and review the way to write time within the story. Following completion of the stories, have the children pick partners. As each child shares his/her story with the class, his/her partner will demonstrate any times on the large clock for all the class to see. Finish reading the story to see what White Rabbit's date really was.

2 ACTIVITY
Wonderland Estimation

MATERIALS
- wonderland work sheets
- lima beans
- recording sheets

Help the children practice and strengthen their ability to estimate "area." Divide them into small groups. Provide each group with a container of lima beans and a folder with wonderland work sheets for all. For each work sheet (e.g., "White Rabbit's Gloves"), the child records his/her estimate, covers the object outlined with the lima beans, counts the beans, and then records the actual number. Encourage lots of group discussion comparing estimates and ways to improve the next estimate.

3 ACTIVITY
Queen Of Facts Cards

MATERIALS
- 1 deck of cards per group

Use cards in small groups to review the basic addition facts and assist in memorization. The numbered cards have their own value. The Ace cards serve as one. Kings, Queens, and Jacks are magic cards which may hold the value the user designates. Rotating around the small group, each player draws one card from the pack in the center. The player next to him/her draws another card, and if he/she states the sum correctly, he/she may then keep both cards. The game continues until all cards have been drawn.

THE STORY ABOUT PING

by Marjorie Flack

LANGUAGE CONCEPTS
Review – each morning, all day, evening, a long while, late

1 ACTIVITY
Ducks In a Line – Part 2

MATERIALS
- flannel board
- flannel ducks
- number cards
- ordinal number cards
- yellow manipulative cubes (100 per group)
- 100 number boards
- markers

Retell the story using the flannel board, and problem-solve to figure out how many ducks were in Ping's family. What missing facts are needed to solve this problem? Working in groups, have the children make up the missing addends and create an imaginary family for Ping using yellow manipulative cubes as ducks. If the ducks went in line other than one by one, how might they go? Review and extend the concept of odd and even numbers introduced in *Make Way for Ducklings*. Have each group arrange their cubes first in paired even numbers and then in unpaired odd numbers. Follow up this activity with continued reinforcement of odd and even numbers using 100 boards. Color all the even numbers yellow and the odd numbers orange.

2 ACTIVITY
Fishing With Ping

MATERIALS

- 18 fish-shaped crackers per child
- Yangtze River work mats
- recording sheets

Have the children work in small groups telling one another stories about diving in the Yangtze River and catching fish. Model some stories first about fish left after Ping dives, fish caught by both Ping and the fishing birds, and how many more fish Ping caught than the fishing birds. After each child tells his/her story, the others record the corresponding number sentence. Upon completing the session, the children may eat their fish as Ping and the fishing birds would!

3 ACTIVITY
Estimating Rice For Dinner

MATERIALS

- assorted types of liquid measure containers
- rice
- small scoop
- estimation number line

As the boy's mother was about to prepare rice and duck for dinner, she needed to be able to estimate how much rice she would need. Practice estimating how many scoops of rice it will take to fill the various containers. Have the children put their estimates on a hanging number line arranged from the lowest to the highest. Talk about the estimates extensively, and practice some mental math with the children before determining the actual scoops used each time.

BUNCHES AND BUNCHES OF BUNNIES

by Louise Mathews

LANGUAGE CONCEPTS

Mastery – ___ x ___ = ___, total
Review – count the bunnies

1 ACTIVITY
Bunny Arrays

MATERIALS
- 1 inch graph paper
- manipulative cubes or another manipulative to use as bunnies
- scissors
- markers

Read the story through the first time substituting repeated addition sentences for the multiplication sentences. Have each child physically show the groups of bunnies with their manipulatives as the story is read. Now read the story through in its real format and model the first couple of multiplication sentences as bunny arrays on the graph paper. Encourage the children to do the same and have them observe that multiplication is repeated addition of equal groups. Complete the activity by having the children color each of the arrays from the story, cut them out, and compare them closely in small groups to see the pattern of how they grew and changed.

2 ACTIVITY
Bunny Stories

MATERIALS
- writing paper
- markers

Model a brief bunny story using one case of repeated addition and ending with a multiplication sentence. *Example: Three bunnies ate ice cream cones. Three bunnies ate hot dogs. Three bunnies stood on their heads. 3 x 3 = 9 bunnies in all. Have each child write and illustrate a bunny story as modeled. Share the results as a class.*

THE FUNNY LITTLE WOMAN

by Arlene Mosel

LANGUAGE CONCEPTS

Exposure – long ago, richest woman in all Japan
Mastery – three minutes ago; two minutes ago;
one minute ago; one grain became two,
two became four; etc.
Review – one morning

1 ACTIVITY
Minutes Ago

MATERIALS

- egg timer (with sand)
- alarm timer

The folktale references the dumplings rolling by three minutes ago, then two minutes ago, and finally one minute ago. Strengthen the children's concept of these times by using both a traditional egg timer where the children can watch the sand fall to the bottom and an alarm timer set for each particular time. This way the children may watch the full three minutes as well as hear the alarm sound at intervals of one minute, two minutes, and three minutes. Following these observations, allow the children to use both timers throughout the day and record activities which take about one minute, two minutes, and three minutes.

2 ACTIVITY
Magic Paddle Rice

MATERIALS

- large cooking pot (1 per group)
- paddle for stirring (1 per group)
- rice
- 3 blank 100 boards

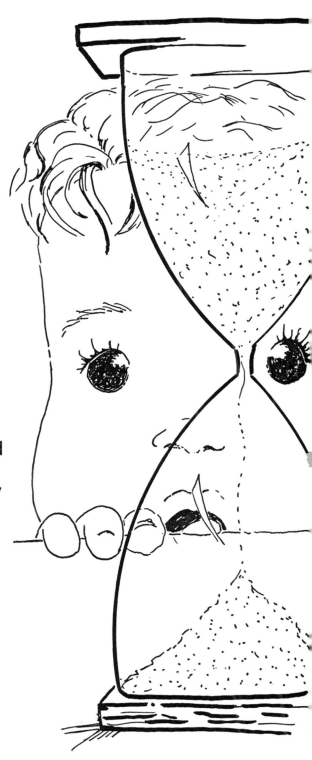

Working in groups, allow the children to reenact the scene from the tale where the funny little woman first cooks rice for the wicked Oni. One grain of rice must turn into two, two becomes four, then four becomes eight, and so on. As this occurs, one member of the group records these numbers on the blank number boards with a marker. Then each group must analyze the pattern on the boards to determine what is "magic" about the pattern. They should be able to see that each number is doubled and that each doubled number is also a number times two.

3 ACTIVITY
How Much Water Did The Oni Drink?

MATERIALS
- metric liquid measure containers
- pint and quart containers
- water
- hanging number line (string or yarn)
- small paper for estimates

This is a good time to extend the children's concept of liquid measurement to include metric measurement. Recall with the class how much blood was in the body of a small child, an older child, and an adult. Compare the amounts of water contained in pints and quarts with that held by liters and half-liters. Allow ample time to experiment with pouring the water back and forth between the two types of measurement. Now have the children discuss how much water the Oni might have drunk from the river. Have them put their best estimate on the hanging number line, and then discuss which estimates are reasonable. The estimates may use any of the liquid measurements introduced thus far.

RESOURCES

Children's Resources

Alice's Adventures in Wonderland : The Ultimate Adventure. Bantam Publishers, New York, 1989.

Bate, Lucy. *Little Rabbit's Loose Tooth.* Crown Publishers Inc., New York, 1975.

Berenstain, Jan and Stan. *The Berenstain Bears' Trouble with Money.* Random House Inc., New York, 1983.

Caple, Kathy. *The Biggest Nose.* Houghton Mifflin Company, Boston, 1985.

Carle, Eric. *The Grouchy Ladybug.* Crowel Junior Books, New York, 1977.

Coleridge, Sara. *January Brings the Snow.* Little Simon, 1987.

Flack, Marjorie. *The Story About Ping.* Penguin, New York, 1977.

Gibbons, Gail. *The Post Office Book.* Harper and Row, New York, 1982.

Guthrie, Donna. *The Witch Who Lives Down The Hall.* HBJ Press, New York, 1985.

Gretz, Susanna. *Teddy Bears Cure a Cold.* Macmillan, 1984.

Hoban, Russell. *A Bargain for Frances.* Harper & Row, Publishers, Inc., New York, 1970.

Hoban, Russell. *A Birthday for Frances.* Harper & Row, Publishers, Inc., New York, 1976.

Kellogg, Steven. *Johnny Appleseed.* Morrow Junior Books, New York, 1988.

Lauber, Patricia. *Get Ready For Robots.* Crowell Junior Books, New York, 1987.

Lloyd, David. *The Stopwatch.* Harper and Row, New York, 1986.

Marshall, James. *Willis.* Houghton Mifflin Company, Boston, 1974.

Mathews, Louise. *Bunches and Bunches of Bunnies.* Putnam Publishing Group, 1978.

McCloskey, Robert. *Make Way for Ducklings.* Viking Press, New York, 1941.

Mosel, Arlene. *The Funny Little Woman.* E. P. Dutton, New York, 1973.

Most, Bernard. *The Littlest Dinosaurs.* Harcourt Brace Jovanovich, New York, 1989.

Pluckrose, Henry. *Time.* Watts, New York, 1988.

Rey, H.A. *Curious George.* Houghton Mifflin, Boston, 1941.

Rockwell, Anne. *Our Garage Sale.* Greenwillow Books, New York, 1984.

Rogers, Fred. *Going to the Doctor.* Putnam, New York, 1986.

Schwartz, David. *How Much is a Million?* Lothrop, 1985.

Shepperson, Rob. *The Sandman.* Farrrar, Straus and Giroux, New York, 1990.

Showers, Paul. *A Drop of Blood.* Harper and Row, New York, 1967.

Slate, Joseph. *How Little Porcupine Played Christmas.* Harper and Row, New York, 1988.

Steig, William. *Sylvester and the Magic Pebble.* Simon and Schuster Inc., New York, 1969.

The Twelve Days of Christmas. Putnam Publishing Group, New York, 1990.

Titherington, Jeannie. *Pumpkin, Pumpkin.* Greenwillow Books, New York, 1986.

Waters, Kate and Slovenz-Low, Madeline. *Lion Dancer – Ernie Wan's Chinese New Year.* Scholastic, Inc., 1990.

Wittman, Sally. *The Boy Who Hated Valentine's Day.* Harper and Row, New York, 1987.

TEACHER'S RESOURCES

Arbuthnot, May Hill. *Children and Books.* Scott Foresman, New York, 1964.

Association for Supervision and Curriculum Development. *Strategic Thinking and Learning: Cognitive Instruction in the Content Areas.* ASCD, Alexandria, VA, 1987.

Children's Books in Print (1985-1986) Subject Guide. R.R. Bowker Co., New York, 1986.

Dreyer, Sharon S. *The Bookfinder – When Kids Need Books.* New York, 1985.

Eakin, Mary K. *Subject Index to Books for Primary Grades.* American Library Association, 1967.

Johnson, Sickels, and Sayers. *Anthology of Children's Literature.* Houghton Mifflin, New York, 1970.

Kamii, C. *Young Children Reinvent Arithmetic.* Teacher's College Press, Columbia University, New York, 1985.

McCracken, J.B. *More than 1, 2, 3: The Real Basics of Mathematics.* NAEYC, Washington, DC, 1987.

National Council of Teachers of Mathematics Staff. *An Agenda for Action: Recommendations for School Mathematics of the 1980's.* NAEYC, Washington, DC., 1980.

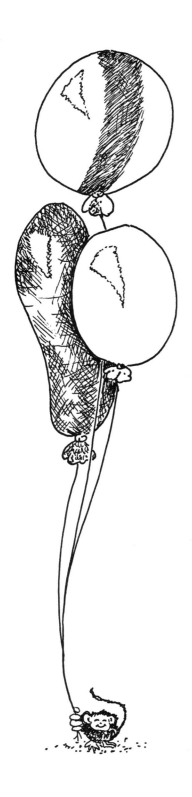